TAGINES

LAKELAND

Lakeland and ACP Magazines Ltd
hereby exclude all liability to the extent
permitted by law for any errors or
omission in this book and for any loss,
damage or expense (whether direct or
indirect) suffered by a third party relying
on any information contained in this book.

This book was created in 2010 for
Lakeland by AWW Books,
an imprint of Octopus Publishing Group
Ltd, based on materials licensed to it
by ACP Magazines Ltd, a division of
PBL Media Pty Limited.

54 Park St, Sydney
GPO Box 4088, Sydney, NSW 2001
phone (02) 9282 8618; fax (02) 9267 9438
acpbooks@acpmagazines.com.au;
www.acpbooks.com.au

OCTOPUS PUBLISHING GROUP
Design – Chris Bell
Food Director - Pamela Clark

Published for Lakeland in the United
Kingdom by Octopus Publishing Group
Limited

Endeavour House
189 Shaftesbury Avenue
London WC2H 8JY
United Kingdom
phone + 44 (0) 207 632 5400;
fax + 44 (0) 207 632 5405
aww@octopusbooks.co.uk;
www.octopusbooks.co.uk
www.australian-womens-weekly.com

Printed and bound in China

A catalogue record for this book is
available from the British Library.

ISBN 978-1-907428-15-9

Additional images: pages 36–7 Fotalia/
Mohamed El Hajjami; pages 48–9 Fotalia/
KaYann

The Department of Health advises that
eggs should not be consumed raw.
This book contains some dishes made
with raw or lightly cooked eggs. It is
prudent for vulnerable people such as
pregnant and nursing mothers, invalids,
the elderly, babies and young children to
avoid uncooked or lightly cooked dishes
made with eggs. Once prepared, these
dishes should be kept refrigerated and
used promptly.

This book also includes dishes made with
nuts and nut derivatives. It is advisable
for those with known allergic reactions to
nuts and nut derivatives and those who
may be potentially vulnerable to these
allergies, such as pregnant and nursing
mothers, invalids, the elderly, babies and
children to avoid dishes made with nuts
and nut oils. It is also prudent to check the
labels of pre-prepared ingredients for the
possible inclusion of nut derivatives.

Some of the recipes in this book have
appeared in other publications.

TAGINES

Rich, aromatic, spicy and authentic, take a journey into the rich world of tagine cookery. Bringing the fragrant dishes of North Africa and the Mediterranean to your kitchen, these 51 recipes conjure up a feast of exotic flavours – classic lamb, chicken and vegetable tagines; quick and easy side dishes, salads, pastries, soups and more.

One of an exciting new series of cookbooks from Lakeland, *Tagines* is packed with delicious colour photos and expert hints, tips and techniques for beginners and experienced cooks alike.

With every recipe triple-tested® for perfect results, these excellent cookbooks are sure to be some of the best-loved on your kitchen bookshelf. To discover the rest of the range, together with our unrivalled selection of creative kitchenware, visit one of our friendly Lakeland stores or shop online at www.lakeland.co.uk.

CONTENTS

THE CUISINE OF NORTH AFRICA 6

MEAT TAGINES 8

POULTRY TAGINES 22

VEGETABLE TAGINES 36

STARTERS & SOUPS 48

SALADS 82

ACCOMPANIMENTS 106

GLOSSARY 124

INDEX 126

CONVERSION CHARTS 128

THE CUISINE OF NORTH AFRICA

North African food, with its heady blend of spices, herbs and fresh ingredients, is a feast for the senses. The region incorporates Algeria, Egypt, Morocco, Tunisia and Libya – countries united by similar ingredients but each with their own distinctive style of cuisine and food customs. Dishes tend to be very highly seasoned in Algeria and Morocco, but spiced in a more subtle way in Morocco, where preserved lemon is used widely. Libyan food is comparatively simple but, nonetheless, delicious.

Food is always served in abundance as family life and the tradition of hospitality frequently result in large numbers of people being together for meals.

THE INFLUENCE OF HISTORY
The food of North Africa tells us much about the history of the region which was influenced by many cultures including Bedouin, Berber, Arab, Jewish, Turkish, Moorish, French, Spanish and Italian. From the Arabs, for instance, came spices, Carthaginians introduced wheat and semolina while the Turks brought pastries and sweet honey cakes. Fruit-growing and the introduction of vines are an inheritance from French and Italian colonists.

TAGINES
Typical of this region's food is the extensive use of slow cooking and the pairing of sweet and savoury flavours. Prunes, raisins, quinces, honey and dates are frequently found alongside beef, lamb, chicken and vegetables. This is particularly evident in the tagine – a rich stew named after the distinctive pot in which it is traditionally cooked.

The tagine pot is made of clay and is made up of two parts: a flat, round base with low sides and a tall, cone-shaped lid. The base of the tagine serves as both a cooking and a serving dish while the lids acts like a closed chimney, trapping the moisture and circulating the steam and flavours in the pot during cooking.

Traditionally tagines would be placed over coals or on an open flame but you can use tagines at home over a gas flame, on an electric hob or in the oven. For best results, always follow the manufacturer's instructions when cooking with a tagine at home. Of course, if you do not have a tagine you can use a normal casserole dish instead. Whichever you choose, the secret of success with tagines is to simmer them gently for hours until the meat in meltingly tender.

KEY INGREDIENTS
The best-known North African culinary speciality is perhaps couscous, which is rolled grains of

semolina wheat coated with finely ground wheat flour. It is the North African equivalent of pasta and is a vital part of nearly every meal, soaking up the flavour and juices of the main dish.

Couscous can be served warm or cold, as a side dish or mixed with fruit, nuts, salad leaves and other ingredients as a substantial meal in itself. In parts of North Africa and the Mediterranean couscous is embellished with ingredients like orange flower water, cinnamon, sugar, almonds and raisins to create traditional desserts.

Chickpeas and other pulses, which are a good source of protein, are also commonly used. It's worth keeping a few cans in your storecupboard as the tinned variety is just as good as dried and far less trouble than remembering to soak the pulses overnight.

Fresh herbs, such as mint, parsley and coriander, feature prominently in North African cuisine alongside dried fruits like apricots and dates. Another characteristic ingredient is

preserved lemon. This is whole or halved lemons that have been pickled by packing them into jars with salt and lemon juice. Sometimes herbs and spices are added too. The flavour is intensely lemony so they should be used sparingly but they add an unmistakable tangy note to dishes.

The vegetables traditionally used in North African dishes are similar to those found in Mediterranean countries and include aubergines, courgettes and carrots.

SPICE MIXES

No North African kitchen would be complete without spices, such as saffron, nutmeg, cinnamon, ginger, cardamom and cloves. Distinctive spice mixes add both fragrance and flavour to tagines and other dishes. Some of the most popular include:

• **Ras el hanout** Meaning 'the top of the shop', this is a complex mixture of numerous ground spices. The precise blend varies from spice merchant to spice merchant but it typically includes cardamom, cumin, ginger,

cinnamon, cloves, black pepper, turmeric, coriander, nutmeg, chilli and wild herbs. The Tunisian version is generally less hot and is perfumed with dried rosebuds.

• **Harissa** Very popular in Tunisia in particular, harissa is an aromatic and fiery paste made from chillies, oil, garlic and spices. Sometimes dried mint or verbena leaves are included. It is added to couscous, soups and meat dishes and is also served as a condiment

• **Za'atar** This is a dry mix of thyme, oregano and marjoram, toasted sesame seeds and salt. Sometimes sumac and parsley are added to the mixture. It is usually used as a rub for meat or fish dishes.

• **Chermoulla** This is used as a marinade or sauce and is a mix of coriander, parsley, chilli, paprika, garlic, cumin and olive oil. In addition, it may include onion, turmeric and ingredients such as harissa. Traditionally served with fish, it also delicious with grilled meat, roasted vegetables, couscous or rice.

MEAT TAGINES

LAMB & APRICOT TAGINE WITH CITRUS COUSCOUS

250g dried apricots
180ml orange juice
125ml boiling water
2 tablespoons olive oil
900g diced lamb
2 medium red peppers (400g),
    chopped coarsely
1 large brown onion (200g),
    chopped coarsely
2 medium sweet potatoes (800g),
    chopped coarsely
3 cloves garlic, crushed
1 teaspoon ground cinnamon
2 teaspoons ground cumin
2 teaspoons ground coriander
250ml dry red wine
1 litre chicken stock
2 tablespoons honey
2 handfuls fresh coriander leaves
200g low-fat yogurt
citrus couscous
1 litre water
800g couscous
1 tablespoon finely grated
    orange rind
2 teaspoons finely grated lemon
    rind
2 teaspoons finely grated lime
    rind

1 Combine apricots, juice and the water in small bowl. Cover; stand 45 minutes.

2 Meanwhile, heat half the oil in large saucepan; cook lamb, in batches, until browned all over.

3 Heat remaining oil in same pan; cook pepper, onion, sweet potato, garlic and ground spices, stirring, until onion softens and mixture is fragrant. Add wine, bring to a boil; simmer, uncovered, about 5 minutes or until liquid reduces by half.

4 Return lamb to pan with undrained apricots, stock and honey; bring to a boil. Simmer, covered, about 50 minutes or until lamb is tender. Remove from heat; stir in fresh coriander.

5 Meanwhile, make the citrus couscous.

6 Serve lamb and apricot tagine on citrus couscous; drizzle with yogurt.

citrus couscous Bring the water to a boil in medium saucepan; stir in couscous and rinds. Remove from heat; stand, covered, about 5 minutes or until water is absorbed, fluffing with fork occasionally.

prep + cook time 1 hour 20 minutes (+ standing)
serves 8
nutritional count per serving 12.8g fat; 439 cal (1837kJ)

MOROCCAN LAMB SHANKS WITH POLENTA & WHITE BEANS

300g dried haricot beans

12 french-trimmed lamb shanks (3kg)

35g plain flour

1 tablespoon olive oil

2 medium red onions (340g), chopped finely

2 cloves garlic, crushed

2 teaspoons ground cumin

½ teaspoon ground cardamom

½ teaspoon ground ginger

2 teaspoons finely grated lemon rind

80ml lemon juice

2 x 400g cans tomatoes, crushed

625ml beef stock

70g tomato paste

750ml water

750ml milk

340g polenta

2 teaspoons finely grated lemon rind, extra

3 tablespoons finely chopped fresh flat-leaf parsley

3 tablespoons finely chopped fresh coriander

1 Cover beans with cold water in large bowl. Stand overnight; drain.

2 Coat lamb in flour; shake off excess. Heat oil in large saucepan; cook lamb, in batches, until browned all over. Add onion and garlic; cook, stirring, until onion is soft. Add spices to pan; cook, stirring, about 2 minutes or until fragrant.

3 Stir in beans, rind, juice, undrained tomatoes, stock and paste; bring to a boil. Reduce heat; simmer, covered, 40 minutes. Uncover; simmer about 50 minutes or until lamb and beans are tender.

4 Heat the water and milk in large saucepan (do not boil). Add polenta; cook, stirring, about 5 minutes or until liquid is absorbed and polenta softens.

5 Serve lamb mixture on polenta; sprinkle with combined extra rind, parsley and coriander.

prep + cook time 2 hours 25 minutes (+ standing and overnight soaking)
serves 6
nutritional count per serving 15.1g fat; 744 cal (3114kJ)
tip You can use any dried bean (cannellini, butter or even chickpeas) in this recipe.

LAMB & QUINCE TAGINE WITH PISTACHIO COUSCOUS

40g butter
600g diced lamb
1 medium red onion (170g),
  chopped coarsely
2 cloves garlic, crushed
1 cinnamon stick
2 teaspoons ground coriander
1 teaspoon ground cumin
1 teaspoon ground ginger
1 teaspoon dried chilli flakes
375ml water
425g can tomatoes, crushed
2 medium quinces (700g), peeled,
  cored, quartered
1 large courgette (150g),
  chopped coarsely
2 tablespoons coarsely chopped
  fresh coriander

pistachio couscous
300g couscous
250ml boiling water
20g butter, softened
6 tablespoons finely chopped
  fresh coriander
35g roasted pistachios, chopped
  coarsely

1 Melt butter in large saucepan; cook lamb, in batches, until browned. Add onion to same pan; cook, stirring, until softened. Add garlic, cinnamon, ground coriander, cumin, ginger and chilli; cook, stirring, until mixture is fragrant.

2 Return lamb to pan. Stir in the water, undrained tomatoes and quince; bring to a boil. Simmer, covered, 30 minutes. Uncover; simmer, stirring occasionally, about 1 hour or until quince is rosy and tender and sauce has thickened.

3 Add courgette; cook, stirring, about 10 minutes or until courgette is just tender.

4 Meanwhile, make pistachio couscous.

5 Serve couscous with tagine; sprinkle with coriander.

pistachio couscous Combine couscous with the water and butter in large heatproof bowl, cover; stand about 5 minutes or until liquid is absorbed, fluffing with fork occasionally. Stir in coriander and nuts.

prep + cook time 1 hour 50 minutes
serves 4
nutritional count per serving 31g fat; 769 cal (3214kJ)

LAMB, APRICOT & ALMOND TAGINE

2 tablespoons olive oil
1kg diced lamb
12 shallots (300g), halved
1 medium red pepper (200g),
   chopped coarsely
2 cloves garlic, crushed
2cm piece fresh ginger (10g),
   grated
1 teaspoon ground cumin
375ml water
375ml chicken stock
½ teaspoon saffron threads
150g dried apricots halves
1 tablespoon finely chopped
   preserved lemon rind
200g green beans, trimmed,
   chopped coarsely
70g slivered almonds

1 Heat half the oil in large saucepan; cook lamb, in batches, until browned. Remove from pan.
2 Heat remaining oil in same pan; cook shallot, pepper, garlic, ginger and cumin, stirring, until fragrant.
3 Return lamb to pan; add the water, stock and saffron, bring to the boil. Reduce heat; simmer, covered, about 1 hour or until lamb is tender.
4 Add apricots, rind and beans; simmer, uncovered, 15 minutes.
5 Serve tagine sprinkled with nuts.

prep + cook time 2 hours
serves 4
nutritional count per serving
41.7g fat; 722 cal (3018kJ)

LAMB & RHUBARB TAGINE
WITH OLIVE & PARSLEY COUSCOUS

40g butter
1kg diced lamb
1 medium brown onion (150g),
   sliced thinly
¼ teaspoon saffron threads
½ teaspoon ground cinnamon
¼ teaspoon ground turmeric
250ml water
500ml chicken stock
2 tablespoons tomato paste
300g coarsely chopped rhubarb
3 tablespoons finely chopped
   fresh mint
olive & parsley couscous
375ml vegetable stock
300g couscous
30g butter
120g pitted kalamata olives
6 tablespoons coarsely chopped
   fresh flat-leaf parsley

1 Melt half the butter in large deep saucepan; cook lamb, in batches, until browned all over. Remove from pan.
2 Melt remaining butter in same heated pan; cook onion, stirring, until soft. Add spices; cook, stirring, until fragrant. Add the water, stock and paste; bring to the boil. Return lamb to pan; simmer, covered, 1 hour 20 minutes, stirring occasionally.
3 Uncover; simmer about 20 minutes or until lamb is tender. Add rhubarb to pan; simmer, uncovered, about 10 minutes or until rhubarb has softened.
4 Meanwhile, make olive and parsley couscous.
5 Stir mint into stew off the heat; serve stew with couscous.
olive & parsley couscous Bring stock to the boil in medium saucepan. Remove from heat; stir in couscous and butter. Cover; stand about 5 minutes or until liquid is absorbed, fluffing with fork occasionally. Stir in olives and parsley.

prep + cook time 2½ hours
serves 4
nutritional count per serving
26g fat; 794 cal (3319kJ)

BEEF & PRUNE TAGINE
WITH SPINACH COUSCOUS

2 large red onions (600g), chopped finely
2 tablespoons olive oil
1 teaspoon cracked black pepper
pinch saffron threads
1 teaspoon ground cinnamon
¼ teaspoon ground ginger
1kg beef braising steak, diced into 4cm pieces
50g butter, chopped
425g can chopped tomatoes
250ml water
2 tablespoons white sugar
100g roasted slivered almonds
250g pitted prunes
1 teaspoon finely grated lemon rind
¼ teaspoon ground cinnamon, extra
spinach couscous
300g couscous
375ml boiling water
80g finely shredded baby spinach leaves

1 Combine onion, oil and spices in large bowl, add beef; toss beef to coat in mixture.
2 Place beef in large deep saucepan with butter, undrained tomatoes, the water, half the sugar and 70g of the nuts; bring to a boil. Simmer, covered, 1½ hours. Remove 250ml cooking liquid; reserve. Simmer tagine, uncovered, 30 minutes.
3 Meanwhile, place prunes in small bowl, cover with boiling water; stand 20 minutes, drain. Place prunes in small saucepan with rind, extra cinnamon, remaining sugar and reserved cooking liquid; bring to a boil. Reduce heat; simmer, uncovered, about 15 minutes or until prunes soften. Stir into tagine.
4 Make spinach couscous.
5 Divide couscous and tagine among serving plates; sprinkle tagine with remaining nuts.
spinach couscous Combine couscous and the water in large heatproof bowl, cover; stand about 5 minutes or until water is absorbed, fluffing with fork occasionally. Stir in spinach.

prep + cook time 2 hours 50 minutes
serves 4
nutritional count per serving 50.3g fat; 1148 cal (4799kJ)

POULTRY TAGINES

CHICKEN, OLIVE & PRESERVED LEMON TAGINE

200g dried chickpeas
2 tablespoons plain flour
2 teaspoons hot paprika
8 chicken drumsticks (1.2kg)
8 chicken thighs (1.6kg)
40g butter
2 medium red onions (340g),
　sliced thickly
3 cloves garlic, crushed
1 teaspoon cumin seeds
½ teaspoon ground turmeric
½ teaspoon ground coriander
¼ teaspoon saffron threads
1 teaspoon dried chilli flakes
1 teaspoon ground ginger
750ml chicken stock
2 tablespoons finely sliced
　preserved lemon rind
40g pitted green olives
2 tablespoons finely chopped
　fresh coriander
tunisian-style rice
600g white long-grain rice
20g butter
1.5 litres water

1 Place chickpeas in medium bowl, cover with water; stand overnight, drain. Rinse under cold water; drain. Place chickpeas in medium saucepan of boiling water; return to a boil. Simmer, uncovered, about 40 minutes or until chickpeas are tender.
2 Preheat oven to 160°C/140°C fan-assisted.
3 Place flour and paprika in plastic bag, add chicken, in batches; shake gently to coat chicken in flour mixture.
4 Melt butter in large flameproof casserole dish; cook chicken pieces, in batches, until browned. Cook onion in same dish, stirring, until softened. Add garlic, cumin, turmeric, ground coriander, saffron, chilli and ginger; cook, stirring, until fragrant.
5 Return chicken with stock to dish; bring to a boil then cook, covered, in oven 30 minutes. Add drained chickpeas; cook tagine, covered, in oven 1 hour.
6 Meanwhile, make tunisian-style rice.

7 Remove tagine from oven. Stir in lemon, olives and fresh coriander just before serving with rice.
tunisian-style rice Wash rice in strainer under cold water until water runs clear; drain. Melt butter in large saucepan, add rice; stir until rice is coated in butter. Add the water; bring to a boil. Simmer rice, partially covered, about 10 minutes or until steam holes appear on surface. Cover rice tightly, reduce heat to as low as possible; steam 10 minutes (do not remove lid). Remove from heat; stand 10 minutes without removing lid. Fluff with fork before serving.

prep + cook time 3 hours (+ standing)
serves 8
nutritional count per serving 35.5g fat; 807 cal (3377kJ)

CHICKEN, CINNAMON & PRUNE TAGINE

2 tablespoons olive oil
2kg chicken thigh fillets
3 teaspoons cumin seeds
3 teaspoons ground coriander
1 tablespoon smoked paprika
3 teaspoons ground cumin
4 cinnamon sticks
4 medium brown onions (600g),
 sliced thinly
8 cloves garlic, crushed
750ml chicken stock
250ml dry red wine
170g pitted prunes
80g roasted blanched almonds
3 tablespoons coarsely chopped
 fresh flat-leaf parsley

1 Heat half the oil in large saucepan; cook chicken, in batches, until browned.
2 Meanwhile, dry-fry spices in small heated frying pan, stirring, until fragrant.
3 Heat remaining oil in same saucepan; cook onion and garlic, stirring, until onion softens. Return chicken to pan with spices, stock and wine; bring to a boil. Simmer, covered, 40 minutes.
4 Stir in prunes; simmer, uncovered, about 20 minutes or until chicken is tender. Stir in almonds and parsley.

prep + cook time 1 hour
50 minutes
serves 8
nutritional count per serving
28.8g fat; 535 cal (2236kJ)

QUINCE & CHICKEN TAGINE WITH CORIANDER COUSCOUS

2 medium quinces (700g), peeled, cored, cut into wedges
40g butter
115g honey
750ml water
2 teaspoons orange flower water
2 teaspoons olive oil
4 chicken drumsticks (600g)
4 chicken thighs (800g), skin removed
1 large brown onion (200g), chopped coarsely
3 cloves garlic, crushed
1 teaspoon ground cumin
1 teaspoon ground ginger
pinch saffron threads
500ml chicken stock
2 large courgettes (300g), chopped coarsely
3 tablespoons coarsely chopped fresh coriander
coriander couscous
300g couscous
375ml boiling water
50g baby spinach leaves, chopped finely
2 spring onions, sliced thinly
2 tablespoons finely chopped fresh coriander

1 Place quince, butter, honey, the water and orange flower water in medium saucepan; bring to a boil. Simmer, covered, 1 hour, stirring occasionally. Uncover; cook, stirring occasionally, about 45 minutes or until quince is rosy and tender.

2 Meanwhile, heat oil in large frying pan; cook chicken, in batches, until browned. Cook onion, garlic and spices in same pan, stirring, until onion softens. Return chicken to pan with stock; bring to a boil then simmer, covered, 20 minutes. Uncover; simmer, about 20 minutes or until chicken is cooked though. Add courgette; cook, uncovered, about 10 minutes or until courgette is tender. Stir in quince and 125ml of the quince syrup.

3 Meanwhile, make coriander couscous.

4 Divide tagine and couscous among serving plates; sprinkle tagine with coriander.

coriander couscous Combine couscous with the water in large heatproof bowl; cover, stand about 5 minutes or until water is absorbed, fluffing with fork occasionally. Stir in spinach, onion and coriander.

prep + cook time 2 hours 15 minutes
serves 4
nutritional count per serving 32.6g fat; 936 cal (3913kJ)

CHICKEN WITH PRUNES & HONEY

1.5kg chicken
60ml olive oil
1 medium brown onion (150g),
   sliced thinly
1 teaspoon ground cinnamon
pinch saffron threads
¼ teaspoon ground turmeric
2 teaspoons ground ginger
310ml water
120g honey
120g pitted prunes
3 teaspoons sesame seeds
30g butter
80g blanched almonds
1 tablespoon thinly sliced
   preserved lemon rind

1 Halve chicken lengthways. Cut each half crossways through the centre; separate breasts from wings and thighs from legs. You will have eight pieces.

2 Heat oil in large deep frying pan; cook chicken, in batches, until well browned all over. Drain all but 1 tablespoon of the oil from pan.

3 Cook onion in same pan, stirring, until soft. Add spices; cook, stirring, until fragrant. Return chicken to pan; stir to coat chicken in onion mixture. Add the water; bring to the boil. Reduce heat; simmer, covered, about 30 minutes or until chicken is tender.

4 Remove chicken from pan; cover to keep warm. Add honey and prunes to pan; simmer, uncovered, about 15 minutes or until sauce thickens slightly.

5 Meanwhile, toast sesame seeds in small saucepan, stirring, until lightly browned. Remove from pan immediately.

6 Melt butter in same saucepan; cook almonds, stirring, until almonds are lightly browned. Remove from pan immediately.

7 Return chicken to frying pan; stir over heat until chicken is heated through. Divide chicken and sauce among serving plates; sprinkle with seeds, almonds and preserved lemon.

prep + cook time 1 hour 20 minutes
serves 4
nutritional count per serving 62.3g fat, 888 cal (3712kJ)

CHICKEN & FIG TAGINE

1 tablespoon olive oil
1kg boneless chicken thighs,
    chopped coarsely
1 medium red onion (170g),
    chopped finely
1 stalk celery (150g), trimmed,
    chopped coarsely
2 cloves garlic, crushed
1 teaspoon ground cumin
1 teaspoon ground coriander
1 teaspoon ground ginger
1 teaspoon ground cinnamon
1 teaspoon ground turmeric
500ml chicken stock
150g dried figs, sliced thickly
1 medium red pepper (200g),
    chopped coarsely
1 teaspoon finely grated lemon
    rind
3 tablespoons coarsely chopped
    fresh coriander
35g coarsely chopped roasted
    unsalted pistachios

1 Heat oil in large saucepan; cook chicken, in batches, until browned.
2 Add onion, celery, garlic and spices to pan; cook, stirring, until onion softens.
3 Return chicken to pan; stir to coat in spice mixture. Add stock; bring to the boil. Reduce heat; simmer, covered, about 30 minutes or until chicken is almost cooked.
4 Add fig, pepper and rind to pan; simmer, uncovered, about 15 minutes or until sauce thickens slightly.
5 Stir in fresh coriander; serve tagine sprinkled with nuts.

prep + cook time 1 hour 20 minutes
serves 4
nutritional count per serving 27.9g fat; 584 cal (2441kJ)

CHICKEN TAGINE WITH DATES & HONEY

1kg boneless chicken thighs
2 tablespoons olive oil
2 medium brown onions (300g),
  sliced thinly
4 cloves garlic, crushed
1 teaspoon cumin seeds
1 teaspoon ground coriander
1 teaspoon ground ginger
1 teaspoon ground turmeric
1 teaspoon ground cinnamon
½ teaspoon chilli powder
¼ teaspoon ground nutmeg
375ml chicken stock
250ml water
70g pitted dates, halved
90g honey
80g roasted blanched almonds
1 tablespoon coarsely chopped
  fresh coriander

1 Cut chicken into 3cm strips. Heat 1 tablespoon of the oil in medium saucepan; cook chicken, in batches, stirring, until browned. Drain on absorbent paper.

2 Heat remaining oil in same pan, add onion, garlic and spices; cook, stirring, until onion is soft.

3 Return chicken to pan with stock and the water; simmer, covered, 1 hour. Remove lid; simmer about 30 minutes or until mixture is thickened slightly and chicken is tender. Stir in dates, honey and almonds; sprinkle with coriander.

prep + cook time 2 hours
10 minutes
serves 4
nutritional count per serving
40.2g fat; 683 cal (2855kJ)

VEGETABLE TAGINES

PUMPKIN & SPLIT PEA TAGINE

200g green split peas
1 tablespoon olive oil
1 medium brown onion (150g), chopped finely
2 cloves garlic, crushed
2 teaspoons ground coriander
2 teaspoons ground cumin
2 teaspoons ground ginger
1 teaspoon sweet paprika
1 teaspoon ground allspice
1kg pumpkin or butternut squash, diced into 3cm pieces
425g can tomatoes, crushed
250ml water
250ml vegetable stock
2 tablespoons honey
200g green beans, trimmed, chopped coarsely
3 tablespoons coarsely chopped fresh coriander

1 Cook split peas in medium saucepan of boiling water, uncovered, until just tender; drain. Rinse under cold water; drain.

2 Meanwhile, heat oil in large saucepan; cook onion, stirring, until softened. Add garlic and spices; cook, stirring, about 2 minutes or until fragrant. Add pumpkin; stir pumpkin to coat in spice mixture.

3 Stir in undrained tomatoes, the water and stock; bring to a boil. Simmer, uncovered, about 20 minutes or until pumpkin is just tender. Stir in honey then beans and peas; simmer, uncovered, about 10 minutes or until beans are just tender. Remove from heat; stir in coriander. Serve with steamed couscous, if desired.

prep + cook time 55 minutes
serves 4
nutritional count per serving
7g fat; 355 cal (1484kJ)

CHICKPEA & VEGETABLE TAGINE
WITH COUSCOUS

2 tablespoons olive oil

2 large brown onions (400g),
    sliced thickly

2 cloves garlic, crushed

2 teaspoons ground coriander

1 teaspoon ground cumin

1 teaspoon sweet paprika

2 cinnamon sticks

pinch ground saffron

2 fresh small red chillies, chopped
    coarsely

2 baby aubergines (120g),
    chopped coarsely

800g peeled pumpkin or
    butternut squash, chopped
    coarsely

400g can chopped tomatoes

250ml vegetable stock

500ml water

200g can chickpeas, rinsed,
    drained

2 large courgettes (300g),
    chopped coarsely

6 tablespoons fresh coriander
    leaves

1 tablespoon lemon juice

couscous

250ml vegetable stock

250ml water

60g butter

300g couscous

1 Heat oil in large deep frying pan; cook onion and garlic, stirring, until onion softens. Add spices, chilli and aubergine; cook, stirring, until fragrant.

2 Add pumpkin, undrained tomatoes, stock, the water and chickpeas; bring to a boil. Simmer, covered, 10 minutes. Add courgettes; simmer, covered, 5 minutes or until vegetables are tender.

3 Meanwhile, make couscous.

4 Stir coriander and lemon juice into vegetable mixture; serve with couscous.

couscous Place stock, the water and butter in large saucepan; bring to a boil. Stir in couscous, remove from heat; stand, covered, about 5 minutes or until liquid is absorbed, fluffing with fork occasionally.

prep + cook time 35 minutes
serves 4
nutritional count per serving
24.4g fat; 658 cal (2750kJ)

VEGETABLE TAGINE WITH OLIVE & PARSLEY COUSCOUS

1 tablespoon olive oil

1 medium red onion (170g), sliced thinly

2 cloves garlic, crushed

1 teaspoon dried chilli flakes

1 teaspoon ground coriander

½ teaspoon ground turmeric

1 teaspoon cumin seeds

500g pumpkin or butternut squash, chopped coarsely

2 medium potatoes (400g), chopped coarsely

625ml vegetable stock

300g can chickpeas, rinsed, drained

6 tablespoons coarsely chopped fresh coriander

olive & parsley couscous

375ml vegetable stock

300g couscous

30g butter

120g pitted kalamata olives

6 tablespoons coarsely chopped fresh flat-leaf parsley

1 Heat oil in medium saucepan; cook onion, garlic and chilli, stirring, until onion softens. Add spices and seeds; cook, stirring, until mixture is fragrant. Add pumpkin and potato; stir to coat vegetables in spice mixture.

2 Stir in stock; bring to a boil. Reduce heat; simmer, uncovered, about 10 minutes or until vegetables are almost tender. Stir in chickpeas; simmer, uncovered, about 10 minutes or until vegetables are tender.

3 Meanwhile, make olive and parsley couscous.

4 Stir coriander into tagine. Serve couscous topped with vegetable tagine.

5 Serve with olive & parsley couscous.

olive & parsley couscous For method, see page 19

prep + cook time 40 minutes
serves 4
nutritional count per serving
14.4g fat; 607 cal (2541kJ)

CHICKPEAS IN SPICY TOMATO SAUCE

150g dried chickpeas
1 tablespoon olive oil
2 teaspoons cumin seeds
1 tablespoon ground coriander
¼ teaspoon cayenne pepper
1 medium brown onion (150g),
    chopped finely
2 cloves garlic, crushed
4cm piece fresh ginger (20g),
    grated
2 tablespoons tomato paste
810g canned tomatoes, crushed
250ml water
5 baby new potatoes (200g),
    quartered
10 baby carrots (200g), halved
    lengthways
6 tablespoons coarsely chopped
    fresh coriander

1 Place chickpeas in medium bowl, cover with cold water; stand overnight, drain. Rinse under cold water; drain. Place chickpeas in medium saucepan of boiling water; return to the boil. Reduce heat; simmer, uncovered, about 1 hour or until tender; drain.
2 Heat oil in large saucepan; cook cumin, coriander and cayenne, stirring, until fragrant. Add onion, garlic and ginger; cook, stirring, until onion softens. Add tomato paste; cook, stirring, 2 minutes.
3 Add undrained tomatoes, the water, potato and chickpeas; bring to the boil. Reduce heat; simmer, covered, about 30 minutes, stirring occasionally, or until potato is tender and mixture has thickened.
4 Add carrot; cook, uncovered, about 5 minutes or until carrot is tender. Remove from heat; stir in coriander.

prep + cook time 2 hours
(+ standing time)
serves 4
nutritional count per serving
7.4g fat; 254 cal (1062kJ)

HARISSA & MINT VEGETABLE STEW

40g butter
10 shallots (250g), halved
6 cloves garlic, crushed
2 tablespoons plain flour
500ml vegetable stock
500ml water
1kg baby new potatoes, halved
410g canned tomatoes, crushed
2 tablespoons harissa paste
1 cinnamon stick
6 tablespoons fresh mint leaves
500g yellow patty-pan squash,
    halved
115g baby corn
60g frozen peas
250g cherry tomatoes, halved

1 Heat butter in large saucepan; cook shallot and garlic, stirring, until shallot softens. Add flour; cook, stirring, 1 minute.
2 Add stock, the water, potato, undrained tomatoes, harissa, cinnamon and about two-thirds of the mint leaves to pan; bring to the boil. Reduce heat; simmer, uncovered, 30 minutes.
3 Add squash to pan; simmer, uncovered, 20 minutes. Add corn, peas and cherry tomato; simmer, uncovered, 10 minutes. Serve stew sprinkled with remaining mint.

prep + cook time 1½ hours
serves 4
nutritional count per serving
10.3g fat; 408 cal (1705kJ)

STARTERS
& SOUPS

LAMB CUTLETS WITH
PRESERVED LEMON YOGURT

1 teaspoon cumin seeds
2 teaspoons ground coriander
1 teaspoon ground cinnamon
1 teaspoon ground turmeric
2 tablespoons lemon juice
12 (480g) trimmed lamb cutlets
sea salt flakes and freshly ground
    pepper
1 (40g) preserved lemon wedge,
    rind only, chopped finely
1 tablespoon finely chopped fresh
    parsley
preserved lemon yogurt
280g greek-style yogurt
2 teaspoons lemon juice
1 (40g) preserved lemon wedge,
    rind only, chopped finely

1 Combine spices and lemon juice in a bowl to form a paste. Rub cutlets with paste; cover and refrigerate for 1 hour.
2 Make preserved lemon yogurt.
3 Cook the lamb cutlets on a heated, oiled barbecue (or grill or grill pan) until browned on both sides and cooked as desired. Season with sea salt flakes and freshly ground pepper.
4 Serve topped with preserved lemon yogurt and sprinkled with combined chopped preserved lemon and parsley.
preserved lemon yogurt
Combine yogurt, juice and lemon in a small bowl.

prep + cook time 35 minutes
(+ refrigeration)
makes 12
nutritional count per cutlet
(including yogurt) 4.2g fat; 68 cal
(284kJ)
tip Rinse the preserved lemons well, then remove and discard the flesh, using the rind only.

LAMB & PINE NUT BOATS

2 teaspoons olive oil
1 small brown onion (80g),
    chopped finely
2 cloves garlic, crushed
2 teaspoons ground cumin
400g minced lamb
1 medium tomato (150g),
    chopped finely
1 tablespoon finely chopped fresh
    flat-leaf parsley
1 tablespoon lemon juice
2 tablespoons sumac
3 sheets ready-rolled shortcrust
    pastry
1 egg, beaten lightly
2 tablespoons pine nuts
1 tablespoon finely chopped fresh
    flat-leaf parsley, extra
140g natural yogurt

1 Heat oil in small frying pan; cook onion, garlic and cumin, stirring, until onion softens. Place onion mixture in medium bowl with mince, tomato, parsley, juice and half the sumac; mix until combined.
2 Preheat oven to 200°C/180°C fan-assisted. Oil two oven trays.
3 Cut each pastry sheet into nine squares. Brush two opposing sides of pastry square with beaten egg; place 1 level tablespoon of filling along centre of square. Bring egg-brushed sides together then push the two unbrushed sides inward to widen centre opening, making boat shape and showing filling. Sprinkle some of the nuts on exposed filling; place boat on tray. Repeat process, spacing boats 4cm apart on oven trays.
4 Bake, uncovered, about 20 minutes or until browned lightly and cooked through. Sprinkle with parsley.
5 Serve combined yogurt and remaining sumac in small bowl with boats.

prep + cook time 1 hour
makes 27
nutritional count per boat
8.4g fat; 139 cal (581kJ)

LAMB FILO CIGARS

1 tablespoon olive oil
1 medium brown onion (150g),
    chopped finely
2 cloves garlic, crushed
500g minced lamb
1 teaspoon ground cumin
1 teaspoon ground cinnamon
1 teaspoon ground ginger
1 teaspoon ground coriander
2 tablespoons roasted slivered
    almonds
1 teaspoon finely grated lemon
    rind
1 tablespoon lemon juice
4 tablespoons finely chopped
    fresh coriander
18 sheets filo pastry
155g butter, melted
140g natural yogurt

1 Heat oil in large frying pan; stir onion and garlic, until onion softens. Add mince and spices; cook, stirring, until mince is browned. Stir in nuts, rind, juice and half the coriander; cool. Season to taste.
2 Preheat oven to 200°C/180°C fan-assisted. Grease and line oven trays.
3 Brush 1 sheet of pastry with butter; top with 2 more sheets, brushing each with butter. Cut layered sheets lengthways into 3 rectangles. Press a rounded tablespoon of lamb mixture into a log shape along one short end of each rectangle. Roll pastry over filling; fold in sides then roll up to make a cigar shape. Repeat to make a total of 18 cigars.
4 Place cigars, seam-side down, on oven trays; brush with remaining butter. Bake about 15 minutes or until browned lightly.
5 Meanwhile, combine yogurt and remaining coriander in small bowl; accompany cigars with yogurt and lemon wedges.

prep + cook time 1 hour
makes 18
nutritional count per cigar
11.6g fat; 171 cal (715kJ)

MOROCCAN-SPICED CHUNKY LAMB PIES

2 tablespoons olive oil

2 medium red onions (340g), cut into thin wedges

4 cloves garlic, crushed

2 tablespoons plain flour

1 tablespoon ground cumin

2 teaspoons sweet paprika

2 teaspoons ground cinnamon

1.5kg trimmed diced lamb shoulder

1 litre chicken stock

400g can chopped tomatoes

2 medium sweet potatoes (800g), cut into 2cm pieces

12 sheets filo pastry

50g butter, melted

1 tablespoon icing sugar

¼ teaspoon ground cinnamon

2 teaspoons finely grated lemon rind

2 tablespoons lemon juice

150g pitted green olives, halved

6 tablespoons finely chopped fresh coriander

200g greek-style yogurt

1 Preheat oven to 160°C/140°C fan-assisted.

2 Heat half the oil in large flameproof dish; cook onion, stirring, until softened. Add garlic; cook, stirring, until fragrant. Transfer to small bowl.

3 Combine flour, cumin, paprika and cinnamon in large bowl with lamb; shake off excess. Heat remaining oil in same dish; cook lamb, in batches, until browned. Remove from dish.

4 Add stock and undrained tomatoes to same dish; bring to the boil, stirring. Return onion mixture and lamb to dish; bring to the boil. Cover dish, transfer to oven; cook lamb 1 hour. Add sweet potato; cook, uncovered, further 30 minutes or until tender.

5 Increase oven to 200°C/180°C fan-assisted.

6 Meanwhile, layer six sheets of filo, brushing melted butter between each sheet; repeat with remaining filo and most of the remaining butter. Using top of 500ml ovenproof dish as a guide, cut out six lids for pies, allowing about a 4cm overhang. Brush lids

with any remaining butter; dust with combined icing sugar and cinnamon.

7 Skim surface of lamb mixture to remove any fat; stir in rind, juice, olives and coriander. Spoon mixture into six 500ml ovenproof dishes; top each dish with pastry round, folding in overhanging edge. Place dishes on oven tray; bake about 20 minutes. Serve pies with yogurt.

prep + cook time 2 hours
serves 6
nutritional count per serving
39.5g fat; 798 cal (3336kJ)

OLIVE OIL PASTRIES WITH CHEESES & MINT

375g plain flour
1 egg
125ml water, approximately
80ml olive oil
1 teaspoon salt
extra olive oil, for shallow-frying
filling
200g finely crumbled feta cheese
100g grated hard goat's milk
  cheese
2 teaspoons finely chopped fresh
  mint leaves
2 teaspoons finely chopped fresh
  dill
2 eggs, beaten lightly
freshly ground black pepper

1 In a food processor, combine flour, egg, water, oil and salt; process until ingredients just come together. Turn onto a board, knead gently until smooth. Cover pastry in cling film, refrigerate for 30 minutes.
2 Divide pastry into 4 even pieces. Roll one piece until 2mm thick. Cut out as many 8cm rounds as possible. Reserve scraps. Repeat with remaining 3 pieces.
3 Knead scraps lightly and re-roll; cut out rounds to make 30 rounds in total.
4 Place 2 teaspoons of filling in the centre of each pastry round; brush edges with water. Fold pastry over to form semi-circles; press edges together with a fork to seal.
5 Shallow-fry pastries, in batches, in olive oil until browned on both sides; drain on absorbent paper.
6 Serve sprinkled with extra mint leaves, if desired.
filling Combine all ingredients in a medium bowl.

prep + cook time 1 hour 10 minutes (+ refrigeration)
makes about 30
nutritional count per pastry
8.9g fat; 131 cal (548kJ)

MINI MOROCCAN PIES

1 tablespoon vegetable oil
1 small brown onion (80g), chopped finely
1 clove garlic, crushed
400g minced lamb
2 teaspoons ground cumin
280g can chopped tomatoes
40g toasted pine nuts
2 tablespoons finely chopped raisins
2 tablespoons finely chopped fresh coriander
3 sheets ready-rolled shortcrust pastry
2 sheets ready-rolled puff pastry
1 egg, beaten lightly

1 Heat oil in medium frying pan; cook onion and garlic, stirring, until onion softens. Add mince; cook, stirring, until mince changes colour. Add cumin; cook, stirring, until fragrant. Add undrained tomatoes; bring to the boil. Reduce heat; simmer, uncovered, about 10 minutes or until thickened slightly. Stir in nuts, raisins and coriander; cool.
2 Preheat oven to 200°C/180°C fan-assisted. Grease two 12-hole deep flat-based patty pans.
3 Cut 24 rounds from shortcrust pastry using 7cm cutter; press one round into each pan hole. Spoon lamb mixture into pastry cases.
4 Cut 24 rounds from puff pastry using 6cm-round cutter; top pies with puff pastry lids. Press edges firmly to seal; brush lids with a little beaten egg. Using sharp knife, cut a small slit into top of each pie. Bake, uncovered, about 20 minutes or until browned lightly.

prep + cook time 1 hour
makes 24
nutritional count per pie
12.2g fat; 198 cal (828kJ)

LAMB KEBABS

500g minced lamb
1 medium brown onion (150g),
   chopped finely
1 teaspoon ground cumin
1 teaspoon ground coriander
½ teaspoon ground ginger
½ teaspoon round cinnamon
½ teaspoon hot paprika
3 tablespoons finely chopped
   fresh mint
140g natural yogurt

1 Combine lamb, onion, spices and half the mint in medium bowl; season.
2 Shape lamb mixture into 8 sausages; thread onto 8 bamboo skewers.
3 Cook skewers, in batches, in heated oiled large frying pan until browned and cooked through.
4 Sprinkle skewers with remaining mint; serve with yogurt and lemon wedges.

prep + cook time 45 minutes
serves 8
nutritional count per serving
10.1g fat; 222 cal (928kJ)
tip Soak skewers in water for at least an hour before using to prevent burning during cooking.

SPICY PRAWNS

18 uncooked medium king
  prawns (720g)
2 cloves garlic, crushed
1 fresh long red chilli, chopped
  finely
2 tablespoons olive oil
1 tablespoon lemon juice

1 Shell and devein prawns, leaving tails intact. Combine garlic, chilli and oil in medium bowl, add prawns; toss prawns to coat in marinade. Cover; refrigerate 3 hours or overnight.
2 Cook prawns in large heated frying pan, in batches, until just changed in colour. Serve prawns drizzled with juice.

prep + cook time 20 minutes
(+ refrigeration)
makes 18
nutritional count per prawn
2.2g fat; 36 cal (150kJ)

KOFTA WITH TUNISIAN CARROT SALAD

500g minced lamb
70g fresh breadcrumbs
3 tablespoons finely chopped
    fresh mint
1 teaspoon ground allspice
1 teaspoon ground coriander
1 teaspoon cracked black pepper
1 tablespoon lemon juice
190g natural yogurt
tunisian carrot salad
3 large carrots (540g)
60ml lemon juice
1 tablespoon olive oil
½ teaspoon ground cinnamon
½ teaspoon ground coriander
3 tablespoons fresh mint leaves
35g roasted pistachios
40g sultanas

1 Combine mince, breadcrumbs, mint, spices and juice in medium bowl; roll mixture into 12 balls, roll balls into sausage-shaped kofta. Cook kofta on heated oiled flat plate, uncovered, until cooked through.
2 Meanwhile, make tunisian carrot salad. Serve kofta with salad and yogurt.
tunisian carrot salad Cut carrot into 5cm lengths then slice pieces thinly lengthways. Cook carrot on heated oiled grill plate (or grill or barbecue), uncovered, until just tender. Place in large bowl with remaining ingredients; toss gently.

prep + cook time 30 minutes
serves 4
nutritional count per serving
20g fat; 441 cal (1844kJ)

BUTTERBEAN DIP WITH PITTA CRISPS

1 clove garlic, crushed
3 tablespoons fresh flat-leaf
  parsley leaves
400g can butterbeans, rinsed,
  drained
1 teaspoon ground cumin
80ml olive oil
6 pitta breads, cut into sixths

1 Preheat oven to 200°C/180°C fan-assisted.
2 Blend or process garlic, parsley, beans and cumin until combined. With motor operating, add the oil in a thin, steady stream until mixture is smooth.
3 Place pitta pieces on lightly oiled oven trays; bake about 8 minutes or until browned lightly.
4 Serve dip with pitta crisps.

prep + cook time 16 minutes
serves 8
nutritional count per tablespoon
5.5g fat; 118 cal (493kJ)

HARIRA

100g dried chickpeas
500g boned lamb shoulder
2 tablespoons olive oil
1 large brown onion (200g),
 chopped coarsely
2 teaspoons ground ginger
1 tablespoon ground cumin
1 teaspoon ground cinnamon
2 teaspoons ground coriander
6 saffron threads
3 trimmed celery stalks (300g),
 chopped coarsely
7 medium tomatoes (1kg),
 deseeded, chopped coarsely
2.5 litres water
100g brown lentils
3 tablespoons coarsely chopped
 fresh coriander

1 Place chickpeas in small bowl, cover with water; stand overnight, drain.
2 Trim lamb of excess fat; cut into 2cm cubes.
3 Heat oil in large saucepan; cook onion, stirring, until soft. Add spices; cook, stirring, about 2 minutes or until fragrant. Add lamb and celery; cook, stirring, about 2 minutes or until lamb is coated in spice mixture. Add tomato; cook, stirring, about 10 minutes or until tomato softens slightly. Stir in the water and drained chickpeas; bring to a boil. Reduce heat; simmer, covered, about 1½ hours or until lamb is tender, stirring occasionally.
4 Stir in lentils; cook, covered, about 30 minutes or until lentils are just tender.
5 Just before serving, stir coriander into soup.

serves 6
prep + cook time 2 hours 30 minutes (+ standing and overnight soaking)
nutritional count per serving 15.6g fat; 314 cal (1317kJ)

VEGETARIAN HARIRA

15g butter
1 large brown onion (200g),
    chopped finely
2 cloves garlic, crushed
4cm piece fresh ginger (20g),
    grated
1 teaspoon ground cinnamon
pinch saffron threads
1 stalk celery (150g), trimmed,
    chopped finely
1 medium carrot (120g), chopped
    finely
2 litres water
410g passata
100g brown lentils
100g brown basmati rice
400g canned chickpeas, rinsed,
    drained
2 medium courgettes (240g),
    chopped finely
3 medium tomatoes (450g),
    deseeded, chopped finely
2 tablespoons lemon juice

1 Melt butter in large saucepan, add onion, garlic and ginger; cook, stirring, until onion softens. Add spices, celery, carrot, the water and passata; bring to the boil. Reduce heat; simmer, uncovered, about 10 minutes or until vegetables are tender.
2 Add lentils, rice and chickpeas; simmer, uncovered, about 20 minutes or until rice and lentils are almost tender. Add courgette and tomato; simmer, uncovered, about 5 minutes or until courgette is tender. Remove from heat; stir in juice. Season to taste.

prep + cook time 1 hour
serves 6
nutritional count per serving
4g fat; 229 cal (957kJ)
tip Brown basmati rice is available from most major supermarkets. If it is not available, use white basmati rice instead.

LAMB & BUTTERBEAN SOUP

200g dried butterbeans
2 tablespoons olive oil
3 lamb shanks (750g)
2 medium brown onions (300g),
   chopped coarsely
1 clove garlic, crushed
2 medium carrots (240g),
   chopped coarsely
2 trimmed celery stalks (200g),
   chopped coarsely
500ml chicken stock
1 litre water
400g can chopped tomatoes
3 tablespoons coarsely chopped
   fresh dill
2 tablespoons lemon juice

1 Place beans in medium bowl, cover with water; stand overnight, drain.
2 Heat oil in large saucepan; cook lamb, in batches, until brown all over; remove from pan. Add onion, garlic, carrot and celery to same pan; cook, stirring, until softened.
3 Return lamb to pan with drained beans, stock and the water; bring to a boil. Simmer, covered, 1 hour, skimming surface occasionally.
4 Remove lamb shanks from pan. When cool enough to handle, remove meat from bones, discard bones; shred lamb. Return lamb to pan with undrained tomatoes; simmer, covered, 1 hour.
5 Just before serving, stir in dill and juice. Serve with toasted pitta bread, if desired.

prep + cook time 2 hours 25 minutes (+ standing and overnight soaking)
serves 4
nutritional count per serving 7.5g fat; 203 cal (849kJ)

MOROCCAN CHICKEN & CHICKPEA SOUP

2 tablespoons olive oil

340g chicken breast fillets

1 large brown onion (200g), chopped finely

2 cloves garlic, crushed

4cm piece fresh ginger (20g), grated

1½ teaspoons ground cumin

1½ teaspoons ground coriander

1 teaspoon ground turmeric

½ teaspoon sweet paprika

1 cinnamon stick

35g plain flour

1 litre chicken stock

1 litre water

2 x 300g cans chickpeas, rinsed, drained

2 x 400g cans tomatoes, crushed

2 tablespoons finely chopped preserved lemon

1 tablespoon coarsely chopped fresh coriander

1 Heat half the oil in large frying pan; cook chicken, uncovered, about 10 minutes or until browned and cooked through. Drain chicken on absorbent paper, cool 10 minutes; using two forks, shred chicken coarsely.

2 Heat remaining oil in large saucepan; cook onion, garlic and ginger, stirring, until onion softens. Add cumin, ground coriander, turmeric, paprika and cinnamon; cook, stirring, until fragrant.

3 Add flour; cook, stirring, until mixture bubbles and thickens. Gradually stir in stock and the water; cook, stirring, until mixture comes to a boil. Simmer, uncovered, 20 minutes.

4 Add chickpeas and undrained tomatoes, bring to a boil. Reduce heat: simmer, uncovered, 10 minutes.

5 Add chicken and lemon to soup; stir over heat until soup is hot. Just before serving, stir in fresh coriander.

serves 6
prep + cook time 1 hour 10 minutes
nutritional count per serving 11.3g fat; 288 cal (1205kJ)

MEZZE

PICKLED CAULIFLOWER

750ml water
375ml white wine vinegar
55g table salt
½ small cauliflower (500g), cut
  into florets
1 medium white turnip (230g),
  cut into 1cm wedges
8 baby beetroot (200g),
  unpeeled, cut into wedges
1 clove garlic, sliced thinly

1 Combine the water, vinegar and
salt in medium pan; bring to the
boil. Boil, uncovered, for 3 minutes.
2 Pack vegetables and garlic into
hot sterilised 1.5-litre glass jar with
tight-fitting lid; pour in enough
boiling vinegar mixture to leave 1cm
space between vegetable pieces
and top of jar. Seal while hot.
3 Store in cool, dark place for at
least 3 days before eating; once
opened, store jar in refrigerator.

prep + cook time 20 minutes
makes 1.1 litres
nutritional count per 60ml
0.1g fat; 12 cal (50kJ)

Clockwise from left: Pickled
cauliflower; Mini lamb pies
(page 79); Spinach filo triangles
(page 79); Baba ghanoush (page
80); Tabbouleh (page 81); Hummus
(page 80); Labne (page 81).

MINI LAMB PIES

SPINACH FILO TRIANGLES

1 Process 150g plain flour, 1 teaspoon dried yeast, ½ teaspoon sea salt flakes, 1 tablespoon olive oil and enough warm water until mixture forms a ball. Place ball of dough in oiled medium bowl; coat dough with cooking-oil spray. Cover; stand in warm place about 1 hour or until dough doubles in size.
2 Combine 100g minced lamb, 1 finely chopped tomato, 1 teaspoon each ground cumin and coriander, 1 tablespoon finely chopped fresh coriander and 2 teaspoons coarsely chopped toasted pine nuts in small bowl.
3 Preheat oven to 200°C/180°C fan-assisted. Oil oven tray. Knead dough on floured surface 5 minutes; roll dough to 2mm thickness. Using 7cm cutter, cut 20 rounds from dough; place rounds on tray. Divide topping among rounds, spreading to edge to completely cover round. Bake pies about 10 minutes or until cooked through.

prep + cook time 40 minutes (+ standing)
makes 20
nutritional count per pie 1.7g fat; 45 cal (188kJ)

1 Preheat oven to 200°C/180°C fan-assisted. Oil oven tray. Boil, steam or microwave 400g finely shredded spinach until wilted; drain, squeeze out as much excess liquid as possible. Combine spinach in small bowl with 2 teaspoons sumac, 2 finely chopped spring onions and 1 tablespoon lemon juice.
2 Cut 4 sheets filo pastry lengthways into four strips. Place one strip on board; cover remaining strips with baking parchment, then with damp tea towel.
3 Spray strip with cooking-oil spray; place 1 rounded teaspoon of spinach filling on one corner, 5mm from edge, flatten slightly. Fold opposite corner of strip diagonally across filling to form triangle; continue folding to end of strip, retaining triangular shape. Place filo triangle on tray, seam-side down. Repeat process with remaining strips and filling.
4 Spray tops of triangles with oil; bake, uncovered, 10 minutes or until just crisp and lightly browned.

prep + cook time 1 hour
makes 16
nutritional count per triangle 0.8g fat; 21 cal (88kJ)

BABA GHANOUSH

HUMMUS

1 Preheat oven to 220°C/200°C fan-assisted. Pierce 2 large aubergines (1kg) in several places with a skewer. Place whole aubergines on oven tray. Bake, uncovered, about 1 hour or until soft; cool 15 minutes.
2 Peel aubergines, chop flesh roughly; discard the skins.
3 Blend or process aubergine flesh with 60ml natural yogurt, 2 tablespoons lemon juice, 1 crushed garlic clove, 60ml tahini, 2 teaspoons ground cumin and 4 tablespoons fresh coriander leaves until combined. Sprinkle with chopped parsley, if desired.

prep + cook time 1 hour 10 minutes (+ cooling)
makes about 560ml
nutritional count per tablespoon 1.6g fat; 25 cal (105kJ)

1 Heat 2 teaspoons olive oil in a pan, add 1 chopped brown onion (150g) and 2 crushed garlic cloves, cook, stirring, until onion is soft. Add 1½ teaspoons ground cumin, cook, stirring, until fragrant; cool 5 minutes.
2 Blend or process onion mixture with 2 x 425g cans rinsed, drained chickpeas, 125ml tahini, 125ml lemon juice, 1 tablespoon fresh coriander leaves, 1 teaspoon ground hot paprika and 180ml buttermilk until smooth. Spoon into serving bowl, drizzle with a little extra olive oil, if desired.

prep + cook time 20 minutes (+ cooling)
makes about 1 litre
nutritional count per tablespoon 2.3g fat; 63 cal (263kJ)

LABNE

1 Combine 840g greek-style yogurt and 3 teaspoons salt in medium bowl; pour into muslin-lined large sieve or colander set over large bowl. Gather corners of muslin together, twist, then tie with kitchen string. Place heavy can on muslin to weight yogurt mixture; refrigerate 24 to 36 hours until yogurt thickens (yogurt will lose about half its weight in water; discard water in bowl).
2 Place thickened yogurt in small bowl; discard muslin. Roll level tablespoons of yogurt into balls; place balls on platter, drizzle with 60ml olive oil.

prep time 20 minutes (+ refrigeration)
makes 24 balls
nutritional count per ball 3.6g fat; 45 cal (188kJ)
tip This recipe must be prepared at least 2 days before you want to serve the mezze. Labne will keep for up to 2 months in the refrigerator; pack balls into clean glass jar with tight-fitting lid, cover with olive oil, seal jar tightly before refrigerating.

TABBOULEH

1 Place 40g bulgar wheat in small shallow bowl. Halve 3 medium tomatoes; using small spoon, scoop pulp from tomato halves over bulgar wheat. Chop remaining tomato flesh finely; spread over bulgar wheat so surface is completely covered with tomato. Cover bowl; refrigerate 1 hour.
2 Place bulgar wheat mixture in large bowl with 3 cups coarsely chopped fresh flat-leaf parsley, 2 finely chopped spring onions, 3 tablespoons finely chopped fresh mint, 60ml lemon juice and 60ml olive oil. Toss gently to combine.

prep time 30 minutes (+ refrigeration)
makes 4½ cups
nutritional count per 3 tablespoons 3.3g fat; 43 cal (180kJ)
tip Chop the mint just before assembling the tabbouleh in the bowl as it has a tendency to blacken and go limp after it's cut.

SALADS

BEETROOT, FENNEL & LENTIL SALAD

3 medium beetroot (1.5kg), trimmed
1 tablespoon olive oil
1 medium fennel bulb (300g)
400g can brown lentils, rinsed, drained
100g wild rocket leaves
200g feta cheese, sliced thinly
dressing
125ml olive oil
2 tablespoons lemon juice
½ teaspoon white sugar
2 teaspoons finely chopped fresh fennel fronds

1 Preheat oven to 180°C/160°C fan-assisted.
2 Combine beetroot in small baking dish with oil. Bake about 1 hour or until tender. When cool, peel beetroot then chop coarsely.
3 Finely chop enough of the fennel fronds to give the 2 teaspoons needed for the dressing. Slice fennel bulb thinly.
4 Combine dressing ingredients in screw-top jar; shake well.
5 Toss fennel, lentils and rocket in large bowl with half the dressing. Add beetroot; toss gently. Top with feta; drizzle with remaining dressing.

prep + cook time 1 hour 30 minutes
serves 6
nutritional count per serving 10.3g fat; 226 cal (945kJ)

CHERMOULLA CHICKEN & CHICKPEA SALAD

200g dried chickpeas
4 chicken breast fillets (800g)
1 medium red pepper (200g),
   chopped finely
1 medium green pepper (200g),
   chopped finely
2 large plum tomatoes (180g),
   chopped finely
1 small brown onion (80g),
   chopped finely
2 tablespoons lemon juice
chermoulla
6 tablespoons finely chopped
   fresh coriander
6 tablespoons finely chopped
   fresh flat-leaf parsley
3 cloves garlic, crushed
2 tablespoons white wine vinegar
2 tablespoons lemon juice
1 teaspoon sweet paprika
½ teaspoon ground cumin
2 tablespoons olive oil

1 Place chickpeas in large bowl, cover with cold water; stand overnight, drain. Rinse under cold water; drain. Cook chickpeas in medium saucepan of boiling water, uncovered, until just tender; drain. Rinse under cold water; drain.
2 Meanwhile, combine ingredients for chermoulla in large bowl; reserve half the chermoulla for chickpea salad.
3 Place chicken in bowl with remaining chermoulla; turn to coat chicken. Cook chicken, in batches, on heated oiled grill plate (or grill or barbecue) until cooked through. Cover to keep warm.
4 Place chickpeas in large bowl with peppers, tomato, onion and reserved chermoulla; toss gently to combine. Serve chickpea salad with sliced chicken; drizzle with juice.

prep + cook time 45 minutes (+ standing)
serves 4
nutritional count per serving 21.6g fat; 477 cal (1994kJ)

ROAST GOAT'S CHEESE, PEA & MINT SALAD

80g shelled fresh peas

4 small (150g) celery stalks, sliced thinly

6 tablespoons young celery leaves

1 small frisee lettuce, trimmed

1 small radicchio, leaves separated

3 medium red radishes, sliced thinly

1 medium (150g) red apple, sliced thinly

6 tablespoons fresh mint leaves

220g goat's cheese, sliced

honey mustard dressing

1 teaspoon wholegrain mustard

1 tablespoon lemon juice

1 tablespoon honey

1 tablespoon olive oil

salt and freshly ground black pepper to taste

1 Boil, steam or microwave the peas until just tender; drain. Refresh under cold water, drain.

2 Meanwhile, make honey mustard dressing.

3 Combine the peas with the remaining ingredients in a large bowl.

4 Just before serving, drizzle with honey mustard dressing.

honey mustard dressing
Combine all the ingredients in a screw-top jar; shake well.

prep + cook time 30 minutes
serves 4
nutritional count per serving
14.1g fat; 243 cal (1016kJ)

MOROCCAN COUSCOUS & CHICKEN SALAD

250ml vegetable stock
300g couscous
1 medium red onion (170g), sliced
 thinly
480g shredded cooked chicken
75g coarsely chopped dried
 apricots
80g sultanas
3 tablespoons finely chopped
 fresh mint
1 tablespoon pine nuts
2 teaspoons cumin seeds
180ml french dressing

1 Bring stock to a boil in large saucepan; remove from heat. Stir in couscous. Cover; stand about 5 minutes or until stock is absorbed, fluffing with fork occasionally. Stir in onion, chicken, apricot, sultanas and mint.
2 Meanwhile, dry-fry nuts and seeds in small frying pan over low heat until just fragrant. Add to couscous with dressing; toss gently to combine.

prep + cook time 15 minutes
serves 4
nutritional count per serving
10.5g fat; 628 cal (2625kJ)

WARM CHICKEN TABBOULEH

160g bulgar wheat
500g chicken breasts, sliced thinly
2 cloves garlic, crushed
180ml lemon juice
60ml olive oil
250g cherry tomatoes, halved
4 spring onions, chopped
   coarsely
2 handfuls coarsely chopped fresh
   flat-leaf parsley
2 handfuls coarsely chopped
   fresh mint

1 Place bulgar wheat in small bowl, cover with boiling water; stand 15 minutes, drain. Squeeze out as much excess water as possible.
2 Meanwhile, combine chicken, garlic, a quarter of the juice and 1 tablespoon of the oil in medium bowl; stand 5 minutes. Drain; discard marinade.
3 Heat 1 tablespoon of the oil in wok; stir-fry chicken mixture, in batches, until chicken is browned and cooked through. Cover to keep warm.
4 Place bulgar wheat, tomato and onion in wok. Stir-fry until onion softens. Remove from heat; add chicken mixture, parsley, mint, remaining juice and remaining oil, toss gently to combine.

prep + cook time 30 minutes (+ standing)
serves 4
nutritional count per serving 21.6g fat; 441 cal (1843kJ)

CHICKEN, PRESERVED LEMON & GREEN BEAN SALAD

160g sultanas
250ml warm water
60ml lemon juice
1 cooked chicken (900g)
175g fine green beans, trimmed
2 tablespoons finely chopped
  preserved lemon rind
340g jar marinated quartered
  artichokes, drained
4 handfuls fresh flat-leaf parsley
  leaves
2 tablespoons olive oil
2 tablespoons white wine vinegar

1 Combine sultanas, the water and juice in medium bowl, cover; stand 5 minutes. Drain; discard liquid.
2 Meanwhile, discard skin and bones from chicken; slice meat thickly.
3 Boil, steam or microwave beans until tender; drain. Rinse under cold water; drain.
4 Place sultanas, chicken and beans in large bowl with remaining ingredients; toss gently to combine.

prep + cook time 20 minutes
serves 4
nutritional count per serving
20.2g fat; 477 cal (1998kJ)

SPICE-RUBBED BEEF FILLET WITH CHICKPEA & PRESERVED LEMON SALAD

1 teaspoon coriander seeds
1 teaspoon kalonji seeds
1 teaspoon dried chilli flakes
1 teaspoon sea salt
1 clove garlic, crushed
600g piece beef fillet, trimmed
6 large plum tomatoes (540g), peeled
425g can chickpeas, rinsed, drained
2 tablespoons finely chopped preserved lemon rind
good handful fresh flat-leaf parsley leaves
good handful fresh coriander leaves
1 tablespoon lemon juice

1 Using mortar and pestle, crush seeds, chilli, salt and garlic into coarse paste; rub paste into beef. Cover; refrigerate 20 minutes.
2 Meanwhile, quarter tomatoes; discard seeds and pulp. Chop tomato flesh finely. Combine in medium bowl with chickpeas, rind, herbs and juice.
3 Cook beef on lightly oiled heated grill plate (or grill or barbecue) until browned all over and cooked as desired. Cover; stand 10 minutes then slice thinly. Serve beef on salad.

prep + cook time 35 minutes (+ refrigeration)
serves 4
nutritional count per serving 8g fat; 279 cal (1166kJ)

WARM LAMB TABBOULEH

500g lamb loin, sliced thinly
2 cloves garlic, crushed
60ml lemon juice
2 tablespoons olive oil
160g bulgar wheat
250g cherry tomatoes, halved
8 spring onions, chopped thinly
60ml lemon juice, extra
6 tablespoons coarsely chopped
   fresh flat-leaf parsley
6 tablespoons coarsely chopped
   fresh mint

1 Combine lamb, garlic, juice and half the oil in large bowl, cover; refrigerate 3 hours or overnight.
2 Cover bulgar wheat with cold water in small bowl; stand 15 minutes, drain. Rinse bulgar wheat under cold water; drain, squeeze out excess moisture.
3 Heat remaining oil in wok; stir-fry lamb mixture, in batches, until browned. Cover to keep warm.
4 Stir-fry bulgar wheat, tomato and onion in wok until onion is browned lightly.
5 Toss extra juice, parsley and mint through tabbouleh off the heat; serve with lamb mixture.

prep + cook time 35 minutes
(+ standing and overnight marinating)
serves 4
nutritional count per serving
21.1g fat; 443 cal (1852kJ)

LAMB, LENTIL & SPINACH SALAD

2 tablespoons mild curry paste
60ml olive oil
600g lamb fillet
½ teaspoon salt
1 medium brown onion (150g),
  chopped finely
1 large carrot (180g), chopped
  finely
1 trimmed celery stalk (100g),
  chopped finely
1 clove garlic, crushed
80ml chicken stock
400g can brown lentils, rinsed,
  drained
100g baby spinach leaves
6 tablespoons coriander leaves

1 Combine one tablespoon of curry paste and one tablespoon of oil in small bowl. Rub lamb with curry mixture then sprinkle with salt.
2 Cook lamb on heated oiled grill plate (or grill or barbecue) until browned and cooked as desired. Transfer to plate; cover, stand 5 minutes then slice thinly.
3 Meanwhile, heat remaining oil in medium pan, add onion, carrot and celery; cook, stirring, until vegetables are softened. Add garlic and remaining curry paste; cook, stirring, until fragrant.
4 Add stock and lentils; stir until hot. Remove from heat; add spinach and coriander, toss until combined.
5 Serve lamb with lentil salad.

prep + cook time 25 minutes
serves 4
nutritional count per serving
30.9g fat; 478 cal (1998kJ)

CHILLI LAMB COUSCOUS WITH SPINACH

180ml olive oil

1½ teaspoons sugar

1 teaspoon sweet paprika

1 teaspoon ground cumin

1 small fresh red chilli, chopped finely

2 cloves garlic, crushed

salt and freshly ground black pepper

3 (600g) lamb loin fillets

80ml lemon juice

2 large (360g) carrots, sliced thinly

300g couscous

375ml boiling water

400g can chickpeas, rinsed, drained

75g baby spinach leaves

4 tablespoons finely chopped fresh mint

4 tablespoons fresh coriander leaves

1 Reserve 1 tablespoon of the oil; combine remaining oil, sugar, paprika, cumin, chilli, garlic and salt and pepper to taste in a small screw-top jar; shake well. Place 2 tablespoons of the dressing in a medium bowl with lamb; cover, refrigerate for up to 3 hours. Add lemon juice to remaining dressing.

2 Boil, steam or microwave carrots until tender; drain. Place hot carrots in large serving bowl with half of the dressing; toss to coat.

3 Heat the reserved oil in a large frying pan. Cook lamb for about 10 minutes or until browned all over and cooked to medium. Transfer to a plate; cover to keep warm.

4 Meanwhile, place couscous in a large heatproof bowl; add boiling water and salt to taste. Stand, covered, for about 5 minutes or until water is absorbed. Fluff couscous with a fork.

5 Combine sliced lamb with remaining dressing, couscous, chickpeas, spinach and herbs in same bowl with carrots. Toss gently.

prep + cook time 25 minutes (+ standing)
serves 6
nutritional count per serving 35.5g fat; 647 cal (2704kJ)

SPICY TUNISIAN TUNA SALAD

2 teaspoons caraway seeds
½ teaspoon ground cinnamon
425g can tuna in oil
300g can chickpeas, rinsed,
   drained
1 small green pepper (150g),
   cut into 1cm pieces
40g pitted black olives, chopped
   coarsely
200g cherry tomatoes, quartered
2 spring onions, sliced thinly
2 teaspoons finely grated orange
   rind
2 tablespoons orange juice
1 tablespoon harissa

1 Dry-fry spices in small frying pan until fragrant; cool.
2 Drain tuna; reserve 2 tablespoons of the oil. Flake tuna coarsely.
3 Combine tuna, reserved oil, spices and remaining ingredients in large bowl. Serve with toasted turkish bread.

prep + cook time 25 minutes
serves 8
nutritional count per serving
12g fat; 187 cal (782kJ)

ACCOMPANIMENTS

ROASTED AUBERGINE WITH SPICED RICE

3 medium aubergines (900g)
80ml olive oil
2 cloves garlic, sliced thinly
1 tablespoon olive oil, extra
1 tablespoon finely chopped fresh
  flat-leaf parsley
1 tablespoon finely chopped fresh
  mint
spiced rice
30g butter
1 medium brown onion (150g),
  chopped finely
1 clove garlic, crushed
3 cardamom pods, bruised
½ cinnamon stick
400g basmati rice
250ml vegetable stock
250ml water
40g roasted pine nuts

1 Preheat oven to 220°C/200°C fan-assisted.
2 Cut aubergines into 3cm slices crossways; discard ends. Heat one-third of the oil in large frying pan; cook one-third of the aubergine until browned on both sides. Transfer to large shallow baking dish. Repeat with remaining oil and aubergine slices.
3 Sprinkle aubergine with garlic; bake, in oven, about 20 minutes or until aubergine is tender.
4 Meanwhile, make spiced rice.
5 Drizzle aubergine with extra oil; top with parsley and mint. Serve with spiced rice.
spiced rice Melt butter in medium saucepan. Add onion, garlic, cardamom and cinnamon; cook, stirring, without browning, until onion is softened. Add rice; stir to coat in butter mixture. Stir in stock and the water; bring to a boil then simmer, covered, about 15 minutes or until stock is absorbed. Remove from heat; stand, covered, 5 minutes. Stir in nuts.

prep + cook time 40 minutes
serves 4
nutritional count per serving
33.1g fat; 717 cal (2997kJ)

SPICY ROASTED PUMPKIN COUSCOUS

1 tablespoon olive oil

2 cloves garlic, crushed

1 large red onion (300g), sliced thickly

500g pumpkin or butternut squash, peeled, chopped coarsely

3 teaspoons ground cumin

2 teaspoons ground coriander

200g couscous

250ml boiling water

20g butter

2 tablespoons coarsely chopped fresh flat-leaf parsley

1 Preheat oven to 220°C/200°C fan-assisted.

2 Heat oil in medium flameproof baking dish; cook garlic, onion and pumpkin, stirring, until vegetables are browned lightly. Add spices; cook, stirring, about 2 minutes or until fragrant.

3 Roast pumpkin mixture, uncovered, in oven, about 15 minutes or until pumpkin is just tender.

4 Meanwhile, combine couscous with the water and butter in large heatproof bowl; cover, stand about 5 minutes or until liquid is absorbed, fluffing with fork occasionally.

5 Add pumpkin mixture to couscous; stir in parsley.

prep + cook time 30 minutes
serves 4
nutritional count per serving
9.8g fat; 325 cal (1361kJ)

VEGETABLE COUSCOUS

1 medium sweet potato (400g)
1 tablespoon olive oil
60g butter
4 baby aubergines (240g), sliced
thinly
1 large brown onion (200g), sliced
thinly
¼ teaspoon cayenne pepper
2 teaspoons ground cumin
2 teaspoons ground coriander
375ml vegetable stock
400g couscous
2 teaspoons finely grated lemon
rind
500ml boiling water
410g can chickpeas, rinsed,
drained
2 tablespoons lemon juice
100g baby spinach leaves
3 tablespoons fresh flat-leaf
parsley leaves

1 Chop sweet potato into 1cm cubes. Heat oil and half the butter in large frying pan; cook sweet potato with aubergine and onion, stirring, until vegetables brown. Add spices; cook about 2 minutes or until fragrant. Stir in stock; bring to a boil. Reduce heat; simmer, uncovered, about 15 minutes or until vegetables are just tender.

2 Meanwhile, combine couscous in large heatproof bowl with rind, the water and half the remaining butter. Cover; stand about 5 minutes or until liquid is absorbed, fluffing occasionally with fork.

3 Add chickpeas and remaining butter to vegetable mixture; cook, stirring, until butter melts. Stir in couscous, juice, spinach and parsley.

prep + cook time 45 minutes
serves 4
nutritional count per serving
20.1g fat; 775 cal (3246kJ)

LEMON-FETA COUSCOUS
WITH STEAMED VEGETABLES

600g butternut squash, chopped
coarsely

2 small green courgettes (180g),
chopped coarsely

2 small yellow courgettes (180g),
chopped coarsely

300g spinach, trimmed, chopped
coarsely

500ml vegetable stock

400g couscous

60ml lemon juice

4 tablespoons coarsely chopped
fresh basil

200g low-fat feta cheese,
chopped coarsely

3 tablespoons finely chopped
preserved lemon rind

6 spring onions, sliced thinly

1 Boil, steam or microwave squash, courgettes and spinach, separately, until tender; drain.
2 Meanwhile, bring stock to a boil in large saucepan. Add couscous, remove from heat, cover; stand about 5 minutes or until liquid is absorbed, fluffing with fork occasionally. Place couscous and vegetables in large bowl with remaining ingredients; toss gently to combine.

prep + cook time 30 minutes
serves 4
nutritional count per serving
9.4g fat; 581 cal (2427kJ)

ROASTED VEGETABLES
WITH HARISSA YOGURT

1.2kg pumpkin or butternut
  squash
3 medium beetroot (500g), halved
2 medium parsnips (500g),
  peeled, halved lengthways
400g baby carrots, trimmed
2 medium red onions (320g),
  halved
2 tablespoons olive oil
50g butter, chopped
280g greek-style yogurt
1 tablespoon harissa

1 Preheat oven to 220°C/200°C
fan-assisted.
2 Cut pumpkin into thin wedges.
Place all vegetables in two large
baking dishes; drizzle with oil and
dot with butter.
3 Roast vegetables, uncovered,
40 minutes, turning once. Remove
vegetables as they are cooked;
return trays to oven further
10 minutes or until all vegetables
are browned and tender.
4 Meanwhile, combine yogurt and
harissa in a small bowl.
5 Serve roasted vegetables with
harissa yogurt.

prep + cook time 1 hour
5 minutes
serves 6
nutritional count per serving
17.2g fat, 352 cal (1471kJ)

MIDDLE-EASTERN ROASTED SQUASH, CARROT & PARSNIP

900g piece butternut squash (or
pumpkin), unpeeled, sliced
thinly
1 tablespoon olive oil
4 large carrots (720g), halved,
sliced thickly
2 large parsnips (700g), chopped
coarsely
4 tablespoons fresh flat-leaf
parsley leaves
40g roasted pine nuts
spice paste
2 cloves garlic, quartered
1 teaspoon cumin seeds
1 teaspoon coriander seeds
½ teaspoon ground cinnamon
1 teaspoon sea salt
1 tablespoon olive oil
20g butter
55g brown sugar
375ml apple juice

1 Preheat oven to 200°C/180°C
fan-assisted.
2 Combine pumpkin and oil
in large baking dish. Roast,
uncovered, about 25 minutes or
until just tender.
3 Meanwhile, boil, steam or
microwave carrot and parsnip,
separately, until just tender; drain.
4 Make spice paste.
5 Place vegetables, parsley and
nuts in large bowl with spice
mixture; toss gently to combine.

spice paste Using mortar and
pestle or small electric spice
blender, crush garlic, cumin,
coriander, cinnamon, salt and
oil until mixture forms a thick
paste. Melt butter in large frying
pan; cook paste, stirring, about
3 minutes or until fragrant. Add
sugar and juice; bring to the boil.
Cook, stirring, about 10 minutes
or until spice mixture thickens
slightly.

prep + cook time 45 minutes
serves 8
nutritional count per serving
10.7g fat; 247 cal (1032kJ)

CHICKPEA VEGETABLE BRAISE WITH CUMIN COUSCOUS

200g dried chickpeas
2 tablespoons olive oil
2 small leeks (400g), chopped
  coarsely
2 medium carrots (240g), cut into
  batons
2 cloves garlic, crushed
1 tablespoon finely chopped fresh
  rosemary
2 tablespoons white wine vinegar
500ml vegetable stock
100g baby spinach leaves
60ml lemon juice
2 tablespoons olive oil, extra
2 cloves garlic, crushed, extra
cumin couscous
200g couscous
250ml boiling water
1 tablespoon olive oil
1 teaspoon ground cumin

1 Place chickpeas in medium bowl, cover with cold water; stand overnight, drain. Rinse under cold water; drain. Place chickpeas in medium saucepan of boiling water; return to the boil. Reduce heat; simmer, uncovered, about 40 minutes or until chickpeas are tender. Drain.
2 Meanwhile, preheat oven to 160°C/140°C fan-assisted.
3 Heat oil in large deep flameproof baking dish; cook leek and carrot, stirring, until just tender. Add garlic, rosemary and chickpeas; cook, stirring, until fragrant. Add vinegar and stock; bring to the boil. Cover; cook in oven 30 minutes.
4 Meanwhile, make cumin couscous.
5 Stir spinach into dish with juice, extra oil and extra garlic; serve with couscous.
cumin couscous Combine couscous and the water in medium heatproof bowl, cover; stand about 5 minutes or until liquid is absorbed, fluffing with fork occasionally. Add oil and cumin; toss gently to combine.

prep + cook time 1 hour 45 minutes (+ standing and overnight soaking)
serves 4
nutritional count per serving 26.9g fat; 594 cal (2483kJ)

EGG & CHEESE PIDE

7g dried yeast
1 teaspoon sugar
165ml warm water
2 tablespoons warm milk
300g plain flour
1 teaspoon salt
1 tablespoon olive oil
topping
3 eggs
90g haloumi cheese, coarsely
    grated
1 finely chopped spring onion

1 Combine yeast, sugar, water and milk in jug. Stand in warm place until frothy.
2 Place 75g of the flour in bowl; whisk in yeast mixture. Cover; stand in warm place 1 hour. Stir in remaining flour and salt into yeast mixture with olive oil. Knead dough on floured surface until smooth. Place in oiled bowl, cover; stand in warm place 1 hour.
3 Preheat oven to 240°C/220°C fan-assisted.
3 Divide dough into three pieces; roll each piece to 12cm x 30cm. Brush edges of dough with a little water; fold 2cm border around edges of dough, press down firmly. Fold in corners to make oval shape.
4 Heat oven trays in oven for 3 minutes. Quickly place pide on hot trays; bake pide 5 minutes. Remove from oven; press centre of pide down to flatten. Whisk eggs with cheese and onion in large jug. Pour into the cavities of the pide. Bake further 10 minutes or until set. Cut each pide into eight slices; serve with lemon wedges.

prep + cook time 25 minutes
serves 8
nutritional count per serving
9.5g fat; 232 cal (970kJ)
tip For a plain pide, roll dough into 35cm oval; place on baking paper. Make indents with finger and brush over 1 tablespoon olive oil; sprinkle with 2 teaspoons black sesame seeds. Heat oven tray; lift dough onto tray on paper; bake pide about 15 minutes.

GLOSSARY

almonds
blanched skins removed.
slivered cut lengthways.
artichoke hearts tender centre of the globe artichoke; purchased in brine canned or in jars.
aubergine also known as eggplant. Depending on their age, they may have to be sliced and salted to reduce their bitterness. Rinse and dry well before use.
baby also known as japanese eggplant, these are small and slender. They don't need to be salted before use.
basmati rice fragrant, long-grained white rice. Wash several times before cooking.
breadcrumbs
fresh usually white bread, processed into crumbs.
packaged fine-textured, purchased white breadcrumbs.
bulgar wheat also known as burghul; hulled steamed wheat kernels that, once dried, are crushed into various size grains.
butternut squash sometimes used interchangeably with the word pumpkin, butternut squash is a member of the gourd family. Various types can be substituted for one another.
cardamom can be bought in pod, seed or ground form. Has a

distinctive, aromatic, sweetly rich flavour.
chickpeas also called garbanzos, hummus or channa; an irregularly round, sandy-coloured legume.
cinnamon dried inner bark of the shoots of the cinnamon tree. Available as a stick or ground.
cloves can be used whole or in ground form. Has a strong scent and taste so should be used minimally.
coriander also known as cilantro or chinese parsley; bright-green-leafed herb with a pungent flavour. The seeds are also available dried and ground. Ground coriander cannot be substituted for fresh, or vice versa.
couscous a fine, grain-like cereal product, made from semolina.
cumin available both ground and as whole seeds; cumin has a warm, earthy, rather strong flavour.
dill also known as dill weed; used fresh or dried, in seed form or ground; has a sweet anise/celery flavour with distinctive feathery, frond-like fresh leaves.
fennel bulb vegetable, also known as finocchio or anise. Also the name given to dried seeds having a liquorice flavour.
feta cheese a crumbly textured goat's or sheep's milk cheese with a sharp, salty taste.

flat-leaf parsley also known as continental parsley or italian parsley.
ginger also known as green or root ginger; the thick gnarled root of a tropical plant.
haloumi cheese a firm sheep's milk cheese matured in brine; can be grilled or fried, briefly, without breaking down.
harissa a North African paste made from dried red chillies, garlic, olive oil and caraway seeds; can be used as a rub for meat, an ingredient in sauces and dressings, or eaten on its own as a condiment. It is available, ready-made, from Middle-Eastern food shops and some supermarkets.
kalonji seeds also known as nigella or black onion seeds. Tiny, angular seeds, black on the outside and creamy within, with a sharp nutty flavour that can be enhanced by frying briefly in a dry hot pan before use. Are available in most Asian and Middle Eastern food shops. Often called black cumin seeds. Available in most supermarkets.
mustard, wholegrain also known as seeded. A French-style coarse-grain mustard made from crushed mustard seeds and Dijon-style French mustard.

nutmeg dried nut of an evergreen tree; available in ground form or you can grate your own with a fine grater.

olives

black have a richer and more mellow flavour than the green ones and are softer in texture. Sold either plain or in a piquant marinade.

green those harvested before fully ripened and are, as a rule, denser and more bitter than their black relatives.

onions

brown an all-purpose onion, with a light brown skin and yellow flesh.

red a sweet-flavoured, large, purple-red onion.

white has a creamy white flesh and a papery white skin. Their pungent flesh adds flavour to a vast range of dishes.

orange flower water concentrated flavouring made from orange blossoms.

paprika ground dried red bell pepper; available sweet, smoked or hot. Sweet paprika is available at delis, speciality food stores and on line.

pine nuts also known as pignoli; small, cream-coloured kernels obtained from the cones of different varieties of pine trees.

pistachios pale green, delicately flavoured nut inside hard off-white shells. To peel, soak shelled nuts in boiling water about 5 minutes; drain, then pat dry.

pitta bread a slightly leavened, soft, flat bread. When baked, the bread puffs up, leaving a hollow, like a pocket, which can then be stuffed with savoury fillings. Pitta is also eaten with dips or soups, or toasted to form the basis of fattoush.

polenta a flour-like cereal made of ground corn; similar to cornmeal but finer and lighter in colour; also the name of the dish made from it.

preserved lemon a North African specialty, the citrus is preserved, usually whole, in a mixture of salt and lemon juice or oil. To use, remove and discard pulp, squeeze juice from rind, then rinse rind well before slicing thinly. Available from specialty food shops and delicatessens.

quince a yellow-skinned fruit with hard texture and astringent, tart taste. Once cooked, they turn a deep-pink-ruby-salmon colour.

rocket also known as arugula, rugula and rucola; a peppery-tasting green leaf.

saffron one of the most expensive spices in the world, true saffron comes only from the saffron crocus, that can produce several flowers a year.

sesame seeds black and white are the most common of these tiny oval seeds; a good source of calcium.

sumac a deep-purple-red astringent spice coarsely ground from berries growing on shrubs that flourish wild around the Mediterranean, sumac adds a tart, lemony flavour to dips and dressings and goes well with poultry, fish and meat. Available from Middle Eastern food stores and specialty spice stores.

sweet potato fleshy root vegetable; available with red or white flesh.

tomato paste triple-concentrated tomato purée used to flavour soups, stews, sauces and casseroles.

turmeric a member of the ginger family, its root is dried and ground; pungent in taste but not hot.

yeast allow 2 teaspoons (7g) dried yeast to each 15g compressed yeast if substituting.

yogurt an unflavoured, full-fat cow's milk yogurt has been used in these recipes unless stated otherwise. Greek yogurt is a thick, creamy variety, traditionally made from ewe's milk.

INDEX

A

almonds, lamb, apricot & almond
   tagine 16
apricots
   lamb & apricot tagine with citrus
      couscous 10
   lamb, apricot & almond tagine 16
aubergines, roasted aubergine with
   spiced rice 108

B

baba ghanoush 80
beans
   chicken, preserved lemon & green
      bean salad 95
   moroccan lamb shanks with polenta
      & white beans 13
beef
   beef & prune tagine with spinach
      couscous 20
   spice-rubbed beef fillet with chickpea
      & preserved lemon salad 96
beetroot, fennel & lentil salad 84
butterbeans
   butterbean dip with pitta crisps 69
   lamb & butterbean soup 74

C

carrots
   kofta with tunisian carrot salad 66
   middle-eastern roasted squash,
      carrot & parsnip 119
cauliflower, pickled cauliflower 78
cheese
   egg & cheese pide 123
   lemon-feta couscous with steamed
      vegetables 115
   olive oil pastries with cheeses &
      mint 58
   roast goat's cheese, pea & mint
      salad 88
chermoulla chicken & chickpea
   salad 87

chicken
   chermoulla chicken & chickpea
      salad 87
   chicken & fig tagine 32
   chicken, cinnamon & prune tagine 27
   chicken, olive & preserved lemon
      tagine 24
   chicken, preserved lemon & green
      bean salad 95
   chicken tagine with dates & honey 35
   chicken with prunes & honey 31
   moroccan chicken & chickpea
      soup 77
   moroccan couscous & chicken
      salad 91
   quince & chicken tagine with
      coriander couscous 28
   warm chicken tabbouleh 92
chickpeas
   chermoulla chicken & chickpea
      salad 87
   chickpea & vegetable tagine with
      couscous 41
   chickpea vegetable braise with cumin
      couscous 120
   chickpeas in spicy tomato sauce 45
   moroccan chicken & chickpea soup 77
   spice-rubbed beef fillet with chickpea
      & preserved lemon salad 96
chilli lamb couscous with spinach 103
cinnamon, chicken, cinnamon & prune
   tagine 27
citrus, lamb & apricot tagine with citrus
   couscous 10
couscous 41
   chilli lamb couscous with spinach 103
   citrus couscous 10
   coriander couscous 28
   cumin couscous 120
   lemon-feta couscous with steamed
      vegetables 115
   moroccan couscous & chicken salad
      91
   olive & parsley couscous 19
   pistachio couscous 14

spicy roasted pumpkin couscous 111
spinach couscous 20
vegetable couscous 112

D

dates, chicken tagine with dates &
   honey 35

E

egg & cheese pide 123

F

fennel, beetroot, fennel & lentil salad 84
figs, chicken & fig tagine 32

H

harira 70
harira, vegetarian 73
harissa
   harissa & mint vegetable stew 46
   roasted vegetables with harissa
      yogurt 116
honey
   chicken tagine with dates & honey 35
   chicken with prunes & honey 31
hummus 80

K

kebabs, lamb kebabs 62
kofta with tunisian carrot salad 66

L

labne 81
lamb
   chilli lamb couscous with spinach 103
   lamb & apricot tagine with citrus
      couscous 10
   lamb & butterbean soup 74
   lamb & pine nut boats 53
   lamb & quince tagine with pistachio
      couscous 14
   lamb & rhubarb tagine with olive &
      parsley couscous 19

lamb, apricot & almond tagine 16
lamb cutlets with preserved lemon
    yogurt 50
lamb filo cigars 54
lamb kebabs 62
lamb, lentil & spinach salad 100
kofta with tunisian carrot salad 66
mini lamb pies 79
moroccan lamb shanks with polenta
    & white beans 13
moroccan-spiced chunky lamb pies 57
warm lamb tabbouleh 99
lemon-feta couscous with steamed
    vegetables 115
lentils
    beetroot, fennel & lentil salad 84
    lamb, lentil & spinach salad 100

M
mezze 78–81
middle-eastern roasted squash, carrot
    & parsnip 119
mini lamb pies 79
mini moroccan pies 61
mint
    harissa & mint vegetable stew 46
    olive oil pastries with cheeses &
        mint 58
    roast goat's cheese, pea & mint
        salad 88
moroccan chicken & chickpea soup 77
moroccan couscous & chicken salad 91
moroccan lamb shanks with polenta &
    white beans 13
moroccan-spiced chunky lamb pies 57

O
olive oil pastries with cheeses & mint 58
olives
    chicken, olive & preserved lemon
        tagine 24
    lamb & rhubarb tagine with olive &
        parsley couscous 19
    vegetable tagine with olive & parsley
        couscous 42

P
parsley
    lamb & rhubarb tagine with olive &
        parsley couscous 19

vegetable tagine with olive & parsley
    couscous 42
parsnips, middle-eastern roasted
    squash, carrot & parsnip 119
peas, roast goat's cheese, pea & mint
    salad 88
pickled cauliflower 78
pies
    mini lamb pies 79
    moroccan-spiced chunky lamb
        pies 57
pide, egg & cheese pide 123
pine nuts, lamb & pine nut boats 53
pistachios, lamb & quince tagine with
    pistachio couscous 14
pitta, butterbean dip with pitta crisps 69
polenta, moroccan lamb shanks with
    polenta & white beans 13
prawns, spicy prawns 65
preserved lemons
    chicken, olive & preserved lemon
        tagine 24
    chicken, preserved lemon & green
        bean salad 95
    lamb cutlets with preserved lemon
        yogurt 50
    spice-rubbed beef fillet with chickpea
        & preserved lemon salad 96
prunes
    chicken, cinnamon & prune tagine 27
    chicken with prunes & honey 31
pumpkin
    pumpkin & split pea tagine 38
    spicy roasted pumpkin couscous 111

Q
quinces
    lamb & quince tagine with pistachio
        couscous 14
    quince & chicken tagine with
        coriander couscous 28

R
rhubarb, lamb & rhubarb tagine with
    olive & parsley couscous 19
rice, roasted aubergine with spiced rice
    108
roast goat's cheese, pea & mint
    salad 88
roasted aubergine with spiced
    rice 108

roasted vegetables with harissa yogurt
    116

S
soups
    harira 70
    lamb & butterbean soup 74
    moroccan chicken & chickpea soup
        77
    vegetarian harira 73
spice-rubbed beef fillet with chickpea &
    preserved lemon salad 96
spicy prawns 65
spicy roasted pumpkin couscous 111
spicy tunisian tuna salad 104
spinach
    chilli lamb couscous with spinach
        103
    lamb, lentil & spinach salad 100
    spinach filo triangles 70
split peas, pumpkin & split pea tagine
    38
squashes, middle-eastern roasted
    squash, carrot & parsnip 119

T
tabbouleh 81
    warm chicken tabbouleh 92
    warm lamb tabbouleh 99
tuna, spicy tunisian tuna salad 104

V
vegetables
    roasted vegetables with harissa
        yogurt 116
    vegetable couscous 112
    vegetable tagine with olive & parsley
        couscous 42
    vegetarian harira 73

W
warm chicken tabbouleh 92
warm lamb tabbouleh 99

Y
yogurt
    lamb cutlets with preserved lemon
        yogurt 50
    roasted vegetables with harissa
        yogurt 116

CONVERSION CHARTS

measures

One metric tablespoon holds 20ml; one metric teaspoon holds 5ml.

All cup and spoon measurements are level. The most accurate way of measuring dry ingredients is to weigh them. When measuring liquids, use a clear glass or plastic jug with metric markings.

We use large eggs with an average weight of 60g.

dry measures

METRIC	IMPERIAL
15g	½oz
30g	1oz
60g	2oz
90g	3oz
125g	4oz (¼lb)
155g	5oz
185g	6oz
220g	7oz
250g	8oz (½lb)
280g	9oz
315g	10oz
345g	11oz
375g	12oz (¾lb)
410g	13oz
440g	14oz
470g	15oz
500g	16oz (1lb)
750g	24oz (1½lb)
1kg	32oz (2lb)

liquid measures

METRIC	IMPERIAL
30ml	1 fluid oz
60ml	2 fluid oz
100ml	3 fluid oz
125ml	4 fluid oz
150ml	5 fluid oz
190ml	6 fluid oz
250ml	8 fluid oz
300ml	10 fluid oz
500ml	16 fluid oz
600ml	20 fluid oz
1000ml (1 litre)	32 fluid oz

length measures

METRIC	IMPERIAL
3mm	⅛in
6mm	¼in
1cm	½in
2cm	¾in
2.5cm	1in
5cm	2in
6cm	2½in
8cm	3in
10cm	4in
13cm	5in
15cm	6in
18cm	7in
20cm	8in
23cm	9in
25cm	10in
28cm	11in
30cm	12in (1ft)

oven temperatures

These are fan-assisted temperatures. If you have a conventional oven (ie. not fan-assisted), increase temperatures by 10–20°.

	°C (CELSIUS)	°F (FAHRENHEIT)	GAS MARK
Very low	100	210	½
Low	130	260	1–2
Moderately low	140	280	3
Moderate	160	325	4–5
Moderately hot	180	350	6
Hot	200	400	7–8
Very hot	220	425	9